What Is Science?

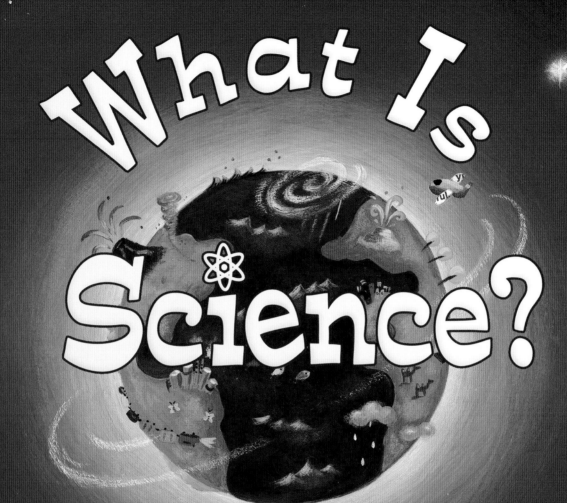

Rebecca Kai Dotlich

illustrated by Sachiko Yoshikawa

HENRY HOLT AND COMPANY ✳ NEW YORK

What is science?

So many things.

The study of stars
and Saturn's rings.

The study of rocks,
geodes, and stones,

dinosaur fossils,
and old chipped bones.

The study of soil,
of oil and gas.

Of sea and sky,
of seed and grass.

Of wind
and hurricanes
that blow;

volcanoes,
tornadoes,

earthquakes,
and snow.

What is science?
The study of trees.

Of butterflies
and honeybees.

Glaciers, geysers,

clay, and sand;

mighty mountains,
and rolling land.

The power of trains,
of planes that soar.

Science is this
and so much more.

So into the earth
and into the sky,

we question the how,
the where, when,
and why.

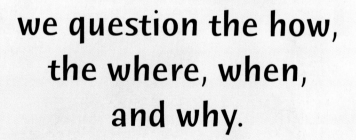

We question,
we wonder,
we hunt and explore

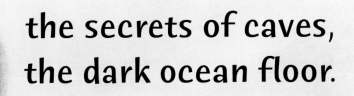

the secrets of caves,
the dark ocean floor.

The oldest of rivers,
the tombs of kings.

What IS science?

So many things!

To Lee Bennett Hopkins—spectacular, forever friend
—R. K. D.

For Tomlinson Fort and my uncle Kotaro Hirata,
with special thanks to Namiko Rudi and Kana Suzuki
—S. Y.

Henry Holt and Company, LLC
Publishers since 1866
175 Fifth Avenue
New York, New York 10010
mackids.com

Library of Congress Cataloging-in-Publication Data
Dotlich, Rebecca Kai.
What is science? / Rebecca Kai Dotlich; illustrated by Sachiko Yoshikawa.—1st ed.
p.   cm.
ISBN 978-0-8050-7394-2
1. Science—Juvenile literature. 2. Science—Pictorial works—Juvenile literature. I. Yoshikawa, Sachiko, ill. II. Title.
Q163.D68 2006   500—dc22   2005020050

First Edition—2006 / Designed by Laurent Linn
The artist used acrylic, pastel, and paper collage on watercolor paper to create the illustrations for this book.
Printed in China by South China Printing Co. Ltd., Dongguan City, Guangdong Province

5   7   9   10   8   6